GROWING TOGETHER IN

TRUTH

CHARACTER STORIES FOR FAMILIES

FAMILYLIFE®
Little Rock, Arkansas

BARBARA RAINEY

GROWING TOGETHER IN TRUTH

FamilyLife Publishing®
5800 Ranch Drive
Little Rock, Arkansas 72223
1-800-FL-TODAY • FamilyLife.com
FLTI, d/b/a FamilyLife®, is a ministry of Campus Crusade for Christ International®

ISBN: 978-1-60200-500-6

Design: Brand Navigation, LLC

Printed in the United States of America
2011—First Edition

15 14 13 12 11   1 2 3 4 5

FAMILYLIFE®
Help for today. Hope for tomorrow.

ORK FOR THE CHURCH

ad when I suffer

s sufferings for his b

ing his church by pro

s message was kept secret

revealed to his own holy

t the riches and glory of C

rist lives in you, and this is your

So everywhere we go, we tell every

m with all the wisdom God has given

in their relationship to Christ. I work

power that works within me.

CONTENTS

WHY TRUTH

One of my favorite encounters in the Bible is between Sarah and God, recorded in Genesis 18:1–15. An angel from the Lord appeared to Abraham, Sarah's husband, and announced that these two senior citizens were going to have a baby. This was stunning news to a man who was one hundred and a woman who was ninety!

Now this had been a private conversation between God's messenger and Abraham. But Sarah, not wanting to miss out, was eavesdropping on the other side of the tent flap. When she heard the declaration that she would have a baby, she couldn't contain herself. She laughed. Though she tried to muffle it, the angel heard.

Sarah had forgotten that God hears all and knows all. He knew that Sarah laughed not because she was happy but because she didn't believe the message. Speaking through His angel, God confronted her. "Why did Sarah laugh?" he asked Abraham (v. 13). Sarah knew she'd been caught. I imagine at that point, like a child found with her hand in the cookie jar, Sarah sheepishly came out from her hiding place. And still like a child, and indeed like all of us, she did not fess up immediately. She lied, saying, "I did not laugh." The Bible adds, "for she was afraid" (v. 15).

The truth could not have been more apparent, but Sarah lied anyway. I have done that, and my children have too. We are terribly broken, we humans.

In kindness and gentleness, God replied to Sarah, "No, but you did laugh" (v. 17). End of discussion. What could she say? Guilty as charged. And the story ends with God speaking the truth to her.

. . .

MATTERS

Our every word is heard and our every thought is known by the living God of the universe. He has called us to be like Christ, who is Truth incarnate. But sadly, the value of speaking the truth, the whole truth, and nothing but the truth is sinking dramatically in our culture. Mistrust, suspicion, and cheating abound. Politicians lie, athletes cheat, corporations falsify, and journalists plagiarize. Some call it "spin," but slick-sounding labels don't change the nature of deception.

And it is ruining our society.

Parents are responsible to teach and train their children to know right and wrong, to recognize truth and non-truth. But knowing the truth amounts to more than keeping a checklist of rights and wrongs. The Bible teaches that the truth must inform our decisions, our choices, and our actions. Truth is not theory; it is the foundation on which we build a life of faith and trust. As Jesus said, "Everyone who hears these words of Mine and acts on them, may be compared to a wise man who built his house on the rock" (Matthew 7:24). There is absolute truth that can be known—the Word of God.

The stories in this devotional are written to teach the value of truth. May you and your family always live according to truth. And may your knowledge of the truth lead each of you to actions that will bring much good to the world in which we live.

Barbara Rainey

TRUTH

MEMORY VERSE

"You will know the truth, and the truth will make you free."
—JOHN 8:32

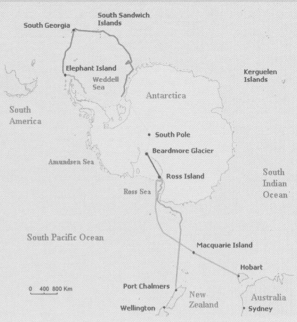

lost and found
truth shows the way

In 1914, twenty-seven men boarded the ship *Endurance* under the command of Ernest Shackleton, bound for the frozen continent of Antarctica. This was Shackleton's second journey to Antarctica; he knew what to expect. Or so he thought.

Five months later and only one day from their destination, the temperatures dropped dramatically. The sea became solid ice and they were stranded for the winter. Six months later— all without sunshine—the men had survived, but their ship had not. Slowly it had been crushed by the ice pack and finally sank.

The men stripped the *Endurance* of her rigging and sails, provisions, and most importantly, her three wooden lifeboats. When the ship sank, they began walking slowly, day after day, hauling their supplies and salvaged hopes of survival across the frozen sea. Finally, in April 1916, with the ice beginning to thaw, they spotted Elephant Island and were able to row to land. After 497 days, they were on terra firma again. But the island was uninhabited; they were still lost.

> Your word is a lamp to my feet and
> a light to my path.
> —PSALM 119:105

Karen found her sextant, the truth of the Bible.

Leaving twenty-two men behind, Shackleton set sail with five others in one of the lifeboats. They headed for South Georgia Island, 750 miles away, with only a sextant* to guide them. An accurate reading of the sextant was critical. A mistake of only one degree would have taken them off course by hundreds of miles. But they trusted the sextant and it guided them safely to their destination. A rescue was launched. Not one man perished.

• • •

Years later a little girl was lost at 25th and Diamond Streets in a sea of concrete. She knew how to find her way home; her problem was she couldn't find her way *out*. The intersection of those streets in inner-city Philadelphia was the hub of the projects. Gang infested and crime ridden, it was as unsafe for a little girl as the frozen ocean had been for the crew of the *Endurance*.

---

*See Reference Points on page 33 for descriptions of certain terms, titles, and historical figures.

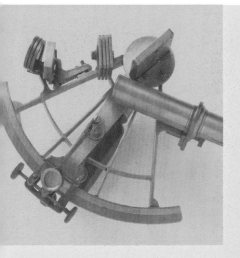

Karen remembers stepping over broken glass and smelling the stench of urine as she would climb the stairs to her apartment after school. Once inside, her home felt like a cage because of the metal fencing that closed off the small patio opening. She was in charge of her little brother because her mother was usually at work. Karen was only seven.

One year later, her mom got married and they moved from the ghetto to a suburb. Though her mother didn't go to church, she insisted that her children attend. So Karen took her brother and walked to the church down the street every Sunday. There Mrs. Green—always dressed in a hat, gloves, and a fine dress—taught Karen's Sunday school class. Little Karen heard words of truth and hope.

For Karen, church was an escape from the tension at home between her mom and stepfather, who seemed to fight all the time. In fact, all Karen had seen of family life was for women to marry young, divorce young, and then move on to the next man. But the people who taught the Bible at her church modeled family stability, and Karen wanted that.

During the summer of her fourteenth birthday, Karen decided to follow God's plan for her life. She heard John 3:16—"For God so loved the world, that He gave His only begotten Son, that whoever believes in Him shall not perish, but have eternal life." Karen recalls, "To know that God loved *me*, that His Son was a free gift for *me* brought great security. I felt so loved, understanding that God wanted *me*, that I could go to heaven, that there was a place there for *me*. I'd been in and out of a lot of different houses over my life, so this promise of a secure place where I could belong forever was my way out of an unhappy childhood."[1] Karen found her sextant, the truth of the Bible.

In college Karen fell in love with a young man named Crawford who came from a fine family. Before she walked down the aisle in marriage, her grandmother whispered, "Karen, if it doesn't work out, you can always come home to me."[2] The first year of marriage was very hard. She was tempted to run back to her grandma, but Karen had told God she wanted to live His way. She was committed to finding answers in the Bible, not her grandma's house.

God rescued Karen because she trusted God's truth to guide her just as Shackleton trusted the sextant to guide him. She believed His Word would set her free to live a better life, and it did.

questions about truth

The Bible says that Jesus Christ is "the same yesterday and today and forever" (Hebrews 13:8). Even though people will change, God never changes. His Word is our GPS.

- Have you ever been lost and needed someone to rescue you? Describe how you felt when you were lost, as well as what it was like to receive help and guidance during that time.
- What are some of the things we sometimes depend on that might not always be reliable?

truth in action

- Go to a library or go online to read more about Ernest Shackleton's adventure to Antarctica. Discuss how the perseverance and eventual rescue of these twenty-eight men applies to the Christian journey.
- Discuss how Karen's life might have been different had she chosen to ignore the teachings of the Bible.

praying together for truth

God, You have always been the Deliverer. As You delivered Moses and the people of Israel from bondage, still today You are able to deliver all who call on You, to set their feet on solid ground, and to set them free. You rescue those who are lost. Teach me to follow You closely that I may not trust my own way but only Yours. Amen.

For further reading about Ernest Shackleton and the *Endurance* expedition, see Alfred Lansing, *Endurance: Shackleton's Incredible Voyage* (New York: Basic Books, 1999).

champion of the cherokee
truth defends the oppressed

A bully is mean to others for no good reason. Usually the bully is bigger and stronger, or at least likes to think that he is. He acts powerful by saying mean things, pushing and shoving, or even hitting. Typically we think of bullying as something that happens in schools between children, but adults can be bullies too. The hunger for power, seen often in adults through manipulative behavior, is motivated by selfishness. The results are always hurtful.

It was a sad day in 1830 when the United States Congress passed a law forcing the Cherokee Indians and other tribes to move away from the land where they had lived for hundreds of years. The path of their exodus became known as The Trail of Tears.

The Cherokee, and many other tribes—the Creek, the Seminole, the Choctaw, and the Chickasaw—lived in the southeastern portion of the United States. Many of them were farmers and cattle ranchers. They built towns, schools, and churches and published a newspaper. Many of them were Christians. In the early 1800s these Indian communities were not bands of criminals

> Teach me Your way, O Lord; I will walk in Your truth.
> —PSALM 86:11

> These Indian communities were not bands of criminals who raided homes and killed innocent people.

who raided homes and killed innocent people; rather, they were very much like their new white neighbors who were moving south by the thousands to establish their own farms and ranches.

But there were powerful men who wanted the Cherokee land. Some held positions as governors, congressmen, or mayors. They were not content with what God had given them and chose to ignore the Tenth Commandment: "You shall not covet" (Exodus 20:17) and the Golden Rule: "Treat others the same way you want them to treat you" (Luke 6:31). These leaders manipulated laws in order to force the Indians to give them what they wanted. They were bullies.

Jeremiah Evarts, on the other hand, was the champion of the Cherokee. A godly man, Jeremiah was troubled that these people, made in God's image just as he was, were being forced to abandon their ancestral homes. The truth of the Bible was his guide, and the Bible spoke clearly about living in harmony with one another. So how could he be silent when the Cherokee were being threatened?

God has children all over the world, and He has a plan for each one. The Bible tells us, "For we are His workmanship, created in Christ Jesus for good works, which God prepared beforehand so that we would walk in them" (Ephesians 2:10). Jeremiah Evarts was created with the gifts and talents to fight for the Cherokee. He was trained as a lawyer, so he understood how to debate using facts and logic. He was a Christian, so he knew God's truth. And God orchestrated his birth at the right time and in the right place for this work to be accomplished.

Those who live by the truth of the Bible, who do as Jesus would do, will not bully others. They will follow what God has given them to do and find contentment in doing God's will. They will seek to live in peace with their neighbors, classmates, and family members. That is what Jesus taught.

Sadly, Jeremiah Evarts' fight to protect the Cherokee failed. The Indian Removal Act,* which passed by only one vote, was signed into law by President Andrew Jackson in 1830, giving him the power to negotiate the Cherokee exodus. The Trail of Tears began in 1838, as the states of Georgia, North Carolina, Tennessee, and Alabama gathered militia to force the Indians to move.

Without compassion, without any love for "the least of these" (Matthew 25:40 NKJV), soldiers burned homes and destroyed and looted property. The Cherokee people were then forced to begin walking west. And it was winter. Thousands died from the cold and starvation. Some were murdered.

Though this story does not have a happy ending, faith in God calls us to hope again. Jeremiah Evarts wrote near the end of his life, "At times I am exceedingly cast down as to the result. . . . It seems a most remarkable Providence, that the bill should pass, when a majority present showed themselves to be . . . opposed to it. This strange state of things should make us stand astonished at the ways of Providence. . . . My comfort is that God governs the world."[1]

The truth of the Bible promises that God will make all things right one day. That is what Jeremiah Evarts believed when his battle to defend the oppressed Cherokee ended in failure. Though the truth does not guarantee success every time, there is a God in heaven who sees all and who is pleased when His children intervene for the defenseless.

questions about truth

- Have you ever been bullied or watched someone else suffer from a bully's behavior? If so, what did you want to do? If you had it to do over again, what would you do differently?
- Think about the Golden Rule—"Treat others the same way you want them to treat you" (Luke 6:31). How does this truth change the way you act toward others?
- When God doesn't make things work out the way we think He should, what are some truths that we can still believe?

truth in action

- Consider specific ways that your family can show compassion for "the least of these" in your community. For example, you could volunteer at a soup kitchen, donate items to a food pantry, or sign up to help at a local charity. Talk to your pastor to find out if you can participate in a church-sponsored mission or community outreach.

praying together for truth

You have made me as I am, Lord. Every detail of size and intellect and talent matters to You. Nothing was by chance. Even my day of birth, my country, my family were chosen by You—all for reasons I will never fully comprehend. But to know that You ordered it all is enough. As the Artist of my life, may You be pleased with how I use the colors You have given me. For the good of Your kingdom, I pray. Amen.

To learn more of Jeremiah Evarts' defense of the Cherokee, see E. C. Tracy, *Memoir of the Life of Jeremiah Evarts* (Whitefish, MT: Kessinger Publishing, 2007).

a grandfather's love
truth corrects lies

In *The Last Battle*, the final book in the Chronicles of Narnia, C. S. Lewis tells the story of Shift, a talking ape who used his cleverness to manipulate others to do what he wanted. One day Shift and his neighbor, Puzzle the donkey, found a lion skin. Shift persuaded Puzzle to wear it and pretend to be Aslan, the Great Lion who ruled over all the kingdoms of the earth. Initially Puzzle was mortified at the thought of masquerading as Aslan, but Shift convinced him it was okay because, he said, the skin had come to them as a sign from Aslan. Puzzle reluctantly put on the lion skin and followed Shift's plan.

As happens when a lie is told over and over again, the story grew and changed. Shift first pretended to be a man. Then, because he wanted power over others, he demanded that everyone address him as Lord Shift, Mouthpiece of Aslan, and he dressed himself in a scarlet jacket and paper crown. He kept poor Puzzle locked in a hut, forbidden to speak, while Shift sat outside and gave everyone orders in the name of Aslan. Puzzle was allowed out only at night so no one could see that he wasn't really Aslan.

> Therefore, laying aside falsehood, speak truth each one of you with his neighbor.
>
> —EPHESIANS 4:25

> For decades Father Zakaria prayed that God would give him a way.

When the real Aslan returned to Narnia, Puzzle finally admitted the truth. Though he had been part of the deception, he was forgiven and welcomed into Aslan's Country. But Shift made no confession and was carried away by the awful god, Tash.

• • •

Around the world today, there are many places where the truth is hidden by powerful leaders who manipulate others by mixing truth with lies. Millions of people who live in these countries are confused and afraid to speak out against those who seem more powerful. But Father Zakaria Botross is not afraid to speak the truth, though his life has been threatened many times. A kind and gentle grandfather, Father Zakaria is an Egyptian Christian, belonging to the group of believers known as Coptics.

Many years ago, Father Zakaria met Jesus Christ and his life was changed. Since that day he has led thousands to Christ with the power of truth, has helped the poor and needy, has preached to thousands, and has seen God perform miracles of healing. His church grew rapidly, but so did his enemies. He was arrested and spent a year in prison, but even there he preached the love of God to fellow prisoners and the guards.

For decades Father Zakaria prayed that God would give him a way to reach Muslims* with the truth of Jesus. Today God has answered that prayer with the far reaching capabilities of the Internet and satellite. Through online chat rooms and a television program called *Truth Talk*, he is able to speak to millions of Muslims all over the world.

At seventy-seven years old, Father Zakaria says his goal is to expose the lies of Islam, a religion that is rapidly gaining converts around the world. Like the tales Shift told in *The Last Battle*, the teaching of Islam often changes as one imam (teacher of Islam) after another issues a new statement of belief. Because Father Zakaria loves his Muslim neighbors, he wants them to know the truth. He says, "My program is to attack Islam, not to attack Muslims but to save them because they are deceived. As I love Muslims, I hate Islam."[1]

He explains that the words of the Muslims' holy book, the Koran, and its teachers mix truth with untruth. But Jesus' words are always truth. Father Zakaria knows the Koran can sound like truth to people because it includes stories about Jesus and Abraham, but he also knows that what it teaches is not the truth but a religion pretending to be true. The ability to tell the difference between a lie and the truth is called *discernment*. Father Zakaria can see the difference because he knows the truth so well.

For bravely speaking the truth, many have called for Father Zakaria's death. Yet he is not afraid. He said, "I fear nothing. My dictionary does not contain the word *fear*. I believe in God and I believe that the epistle of Ephesians says we are created in Christ Jesus for a plan, which was engaged from the early beginning. No one can cut it, and when it is completed no one can continue it."[2]

It is wonderful to know that God has His people all over the world busily working to bring more people into the kingdom of light. Such a man is Father Zakaria, an Egyptian grandfather who knows the truth and is using it to shine light on the lies of a false religion that many might be set free.

questions about truth

- Have you ever seen someone behave like Shift, trying to control others by deception? What happened?
- Have you ever seen someone behave like Puzzle, pretending to be someone other than his or her true self? Why is this kind of pretending a bad thing to do?
- If Aslan were to come to you, would he find you being truthful? What would he say to you?
- Will you be like Father Zakaria and learn the truth so you, too, can recognize lies and half-truths? List a few ways you could learn more of God's truth, such as joining a Bible study group, reading through the Bible, and so on. Then, once you know the truth, will you be brave and loving and correct the lies you hear others believing?

truth in action

- If you haven't read C. S. Lewis's book *The Last Battle*, read it together with your family.

praying together for truth

You, O Lord, are the God of all truth. We are the ones who are confused and bewildered. Help us to seek truth, to live by truth, and to speak truth. Then we will know You more fully and we will be more like Jesus, who is Truth incarnate. Amen.

For further reading about Father Zakaria, see Stuart Robinson, *Defying Death: Zakaria Botross—Apostle to Islam* (Brisbane, Australia: CityHarvest International, 2008), www.vocations4life.com/au/shop/categories /Biography-%26-Inspirational.

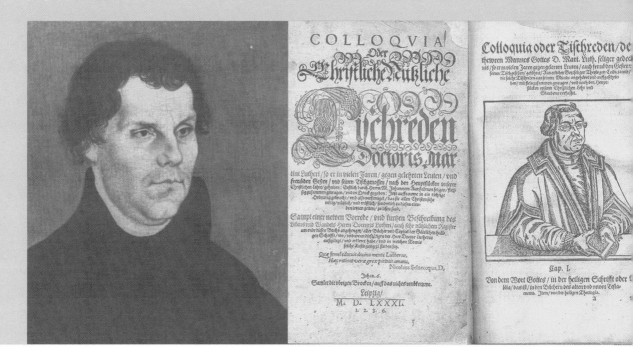

a mutineer and a monk
truth brings freedom

THE BIBLE OF THE "BOUNTY."

HARTFORD, May 21.—In the safe in the Town Clerk's office in Windsor is stored carefully away the "Bounty" Bible. It has been brought to light by the investigations of a young man who has just returned from Pitcairn's Island and who is now in journalism in New-York State. The story of the mutiny on the old ship Bounty and the subsequent settlement of nine of the mutineers on Pitcairn, among the islands of the South Pacific, is a familiar one.

The Bible that belonged to the vessel is in custody of Mr. Levi Hayden, and is in the Town Clerk's office wholly for safe keeping. On the fly leaf is written:

"THE MUTINEERS' BIBLE OF 1789.

"Presented by John Adams, grandson of the patriarch of Pitcairn Island, to Levi Hayden, February, 1839, and held by Peletiah Perrit, President of the American Seaman's Friend Society of New-York from 1851 and given in charge of H. Sydney

Mutiny on the Bounty tells the story of the notorious revolt that occurred aboard the English ship the *Bounty*. The story goes like this: In 1789, the *Bounty* and her crew sailed across the Pacific Ocean on a voyage of exploration. After a six-month stay on the tropical island of Tahiti, many of the sailors decided they would not return to England, so they staged a mutiny. Led by an officer on the ship, the sailors captured their captain and those who were loyal to him and set them adrift in a tiny lifeboat. Amazingly these men survived the thirty-seven-hundred-mile journey to civilization.

But the rebellion did not end well. The sailors kidnapped some women, took others as slaves, and then sailed the *Bounty* to the island of Pitcairn. There they lived lives of drunkenness and murder. Within two years, all the rebel Englishmen, except one, died by disease or fighting.

The lone survivor, Alexander Smith, was the only man left on Pitcairn with the Tahitian women and children. Then he found the Bible, a book that every ship carried on its long journeys. As he

> You will know the truth, and the truth will make you free.
> —JOHN 8:32

How can I know God and have peace about life after death?

read it he began to change. All else had failed him, but the truth of the Bible offered forgiveness and hope, something Alexander desperately needed. Soon he was teaching the truth of the Bible to the women and children. Twenty years later when another ship finally landed at Pitcairn, those sailors were surprised when they found a community of Christians living together in peace and harmony.

• • •

Another man who was changed by the power of the Bible was Martin Luther. One day when he was twenty-two, Martin was returning to his university when he was caught in a thunderstorm. Unable to escape, he was soaked to the skin and nearly killed by a lightning strike that took the life of his friend who was riding with him. Martin was badly shaken. He was troubled that he survived and his friend had died. What did it mean? He began to think more about God and wondered, *How can I know God and have peace about life after death?*

For years after this event, Martin Luther worked hard to please God so he could get into heaven. He even studied to be a monk, someone who devotes his life to work in the church. But despite his good works, he felt no closer to God. Then Martin read a verse that changed him: "The righteous man shall live by faith" (Romans 1:17). Those two words, "by faith," brought him the joy of discovery. "By faith" meant that having peace with God was not something he had to earn.

All of us know that it takes hard work to earn good grades in school. There are also rules to be obeyed in schools, in our communities, and in our homes. We can easily think that the way to please God is the same—keep the rules and work hard, and He will let you into heaven someday. That's what Martin Luther believed until he discovered "by faith." These words meant that faith in God's way of salvation through Jesus Christ was enough—no works, no report card, no "I hope I'm good enough."

In the time when Martin lived, there was a very unbiblical practice in the church. Church leaders taught the people that not only did they have to obey all the church rules, but they also had to pay money to the priests to have their sins forgiven.

One day Martin had enough. The Bible did not teach that sins were forgiven for money! On October 31, 1517, Martin Luther made a list of reasons that this practice, called indulgences,* was wrong and nailed the list on the wooden door of the church. Everyone saw his list as they came to services the next day, All Saints' Day. The church leaders were furious. They did not want to lose the money.

An order was given to burn all the books Martin Luther had written. The church leaders demanded that he sign a paper saying he had been wrong. He refused. Sometime later he was taken before the emperor, who demanded that he recant. Instead Martin Luther replied, "Here I stand, I can do no other. May God help me!"[1] He knew the Bible was the true Word of God. He would stand on the truth no matter what came as a result.

Today, those who believe as Martin Luther did are often called Protestants, a name that began with Luther as he protested against the lies of the church that day in 1517.

questions about truth

- Is there a verse or a phrase from the Bible that has changed the way you think about God and what you believe? Share it with your family.
- When Alexander Smith and Martin Luther discovered the truth of the Bible, they began to share it with others. How can you share the truth with others around you?
- Jesus taught that His followers were not to hide their light, or truth, under a bushel, but they were to let it shine so others could see and also believe (Matthew 5:15 KJV). With whom can you share the truth of the Bible?

truth in action

- As a family, create a list of at least ten people—family members or friends—who need to hear the truth of Jesus Christ. Discuss specific ways you can share the truth with them. Then pray together for each person on the list, asking God to give you the opportunity and boldness to share His truth.

praying together for truth

I confess, Lord, that it is so easy to forget to read the Bible, Your divine words to me. I forget that every word is inspired, alive, eternal, powerful, and able to change my heart, any heart. Your Word, the unchanging truth, will never change or fade away. Help me to treasure Your truth, to read it eagerly, and to be careful with how I handle Your book—to hold it reverently, for it is holy as You are holy. Amen.

For more information about Martin Luther and the Protestant Reformation, see Roland Bainton, *Here I Stand: A Life of Martin Luther* (New York: Penguin, 1995).

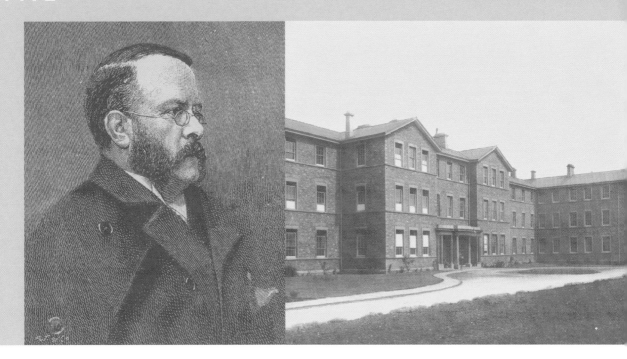

all the children of the world

truth takes action

18

Thomas Barnardo was small in stature—he stood a mere five feet and three inches—but he towered with commitment to share the love of Christ with the street children of London.

He began homes and schools for children, putting a sign on the door: "No destitute child ever refused admittance." As he cared for these little ones, he also started a church to reach the adults with the truth of Christ. Next he went to medical school so he could address the health problems of the children. His wife, a nurse, formed a nursing organization to care for the sick and poor. At the end of his life, Thomas had cared for thousands of children in London and in other towns and cities across England.

As a result of Thomas' ministry—along with the efforts of many other men and women—the plight of the homeless children in England was reversed. But today a similar crisis has fallen on other countries like China, El Salvador, Guatemala, and throughout the continent of Africa. The most recent statistics estimate more than 134 million orphans worldwide![1] Once again the world needs people who will believe God and who will take action to rescue the children.

> Truly I say to you, to the extent that you did it to one of these brothers of Mine, even the least of them, you did it to Me.
> —MATTHEW 25:40

> Once again the world needs people who will believe God and who will take action to rescue the children.

Meet Katie Davis, a nice middle-class American girl. At the age of eighteen she went on a mission trip to the country of Uganda in central Africa. There she fell in love with the people of Uganda, especially the children. The next year, in 2007, Katie returned to teach kindergarten for a year. As she walked some of her students home, she was surprised to see children all along the road. She wondered why they weren't in school. As she began to investigate she learned that schools in Uganda, though government sponsored, still charged tuition. Most families in Uganda were too poor to afford schooling for their children.

Katie took action. By raising money from friends, $300 per year per child, she was able to place more than four hundred children in school. This modest amount of money paid for tuition, books, meals, medical care, and spiritual training.

Katie saw more needs and kept finding ways to meet them. She began a nonprofit organization called Amazima Ministries, which seeks to meet the needs of the poor in Uganda. (*Amazima*

means *truth* in the Ugandan language.) Then she adopted three little girls. Katie wasn't hindered by being single or by being young. Instead she was moved by the needs of these orphan girls, and she knew she could love them.

Remarkably, Katie has continued to do even more, initiating a feeding program for children and a vocational program for women (to teach them to make and sell bead necklaces). She is also planning to start a school. And she has adopted a total of thirteen Ugandan girls!

Katie says, "People tell me I am brave. People tell me I am strong. People tell me, 'Good job.' Well here is the truth of it: I am really not that brave, I am not really that strong, and I am not doing anything spectacular. I am just doing what God called me to do as a follower of Him. Feed His sheep, do unto the least of His people."[2]

Today Katie is twenty-two. Uganda is now her home. She writes in her blog about the glorious journey she is taking with God. In June 2011 she wrote:

We sit in the dirt, not worried about the red stains, and serve 400 plates of food to sponsored children on Saturday. I look into these faces and remember them nearly 4 years ago, destitute and hopeless and starving. Afraid of my funny white skin. We feed them lunch and we feed them God's Word and we watch them transform.

Our family sits on the street corner down town sharing ice cream and laughter. My daughter bends low to offer a homeless man her popsicle and as he cries that no one cares about him she looks straight into his face. *"We will be your family,"* she asserts, and she means it. We kneel on the pavement and we pray and people stop to look but we hardly notice because we were made for this.[3]

Orphans are not just found in Africa, but all over the world. In America most orphaned children are in our foster-care system. Most of them have their basic needs met, but they still are orphans, alone without a family to which they belong.

When we see the truth, really see it, we are compelled to act. Jesus told His disciples, "Feed my sheep" (John 21:17 NKJV). And we are truly His followers if we do what He did.

questions about truth

- In what specific ways can your family help the orphans in your town?
- Are you willing to go wherever God calls you? What do you sense God calling you to do that you may be resisting?
- How would you respond if your son or daughter chose to move to a foreign country to care for orphans?

truth in action

- Go to Amazima.org to read more about Katie Davis and her ministry.
- As a family, consider sponsoring* one of the Ugandan children needing help. Or talk to your friends or church about sponsoring a child (or children) as a group.

praying together for truth

Lord, there is no greater joy, no deeper satisfaction than to be fulfilling the purpose for which You made me. You are the Master, the Creator! To be about Your business—to be changing lives with Your love—is to display Your wonders to a broken world. May Your light shine, O Lord, through me today. Amen.

For further reading see *Kisses from Katie: A Story of Relentless Love and Redemption* (Brentwood, TN: Howard Books, 2011).

for an audience of one
truth stands firm

Just a few years after Jesus went back to heaven, those who followed Him began to be persecuted. In AD 202, the Roman emperor issued an edict against all Christians. Among those arrested was a young mother in her early twenties named Perpetua. Born in North Africa, Perpetua grew up in a prosperous family with the benefits of a good education and a happy childhood. Her mother was devoted to Christ and raised Perpetua and her brothers to love and follow Jesus.

Perpetua was tried and sentenced to execution along with a group of other believers. Her father, who did not believe in Christ, begged her to renounce her faith, reminding her that her baby boy would become motherless if she did not recant. She replied, "Father, do you see this water pitcher? Can it be called by any other name than what it is? So also I cannot call myself by any other name than what I am—a Christian."[1]

On the night before she was to be killed, Perpetua wrote of experiencing God's comforting strength: "I saw that I should not fight with beasts but with the devil; I knew the victory to be

For you stand firm in your faith.

—2 CORINTHIANS 1:24 ESV

It was more important to obey God than men.

mine."[2] The next day, the Christians were marched into the arena. There before a crowd of cheering people, Perpetua and the others were killed by wild animals.*

Perpetua, a beautiful young mother, knew that this life is only temporary and looked forward to the life that lasts forever in heaven. After her death, her chief jailer committed his life to Jesus Christ, so inspired was he by her confident faith. And the truth she died for became an example to her son that he, too, should stand firm in Jesus as she did.

• • •

Almost two thousand years after Perpetua, there lived in the country of Germany a young pastor named Dietrich Bonhoeffer who also paid a great price for his faith. Dietrich was born into a prosperous family; his godly mother taught him and his siblings to love and obey Jesus. Dietrich's father did not profess saving faith in Christ, but Dietrich's life was happy, safe, and secure until

he reached his midtwenties. It was then that Adolf Hitler, the ruler of his country, turned against those of the truth.

As Dietrich and his family and friends learned of the crimes being committed against the Jews and the handicapped, they talked about what they should do. The majority of the Christians in Germany ignored the evil because they were afraid. But Bonhoeffer believed it was more important to obey God than men and that safety on earth was not as important as pleasing God.

After much prayer and careful study of the Bible, Dietrich came to the conclusion that he must help those who were trying to stop Hitler. And for this he was arrested and put in jail. He later wrote about listening to God in difficult circumstances and then following God without reservation. He said that believers must be ready "to sacrifice all" and to be completely obedient and loyal to God alone.[3]

Believing the truth may not always be easy. In fact, it will be extremely difficult at times. Knowing what God has for us is an individual matter. We cannot find God's will by looking to what others are doing.

• • •

One day after the resurrection, Jesus' disciples were fishing in the Sea of Galilee. After returning to the shore, they found that Jesus was there and had already built a fire to cook breakfast for them. After they all ate, Jesus began to ask questions of Peter. He asked, "Do you love Me?" and to Peter's reply, Jesus said, "Tend My sheep," then "Follow Me" (John 21:17, 19). Peter turned his head and saw John and he asked Jesus, "What about this man?" (v. 21).

It is so like us as humans to want to know what Jesus plans for someone else. We want to compare what God asks another person to do with what He asks us to do. But Jesus' answer to Peter is also His answer to us: "What is that to you? You follow Me!" (v. 22).

Jesus asks each one who believes to stand firm in the truth, but He designs our circumstances uniquely. The faithfulness of believers like Perpetua and Dietrich Bonhoeffer cause us to ask ourselves, what will we believe when challenged by hard times? Will we stand firm in the truth as they did? Will we remember that it is God we must please?

Perpetua and Bonhoeffer knew they would stand before Jesus Christ one day and give an account (Romans 14:12). And so will we.

questions about truth

- What does it mean to stand firm for the truth? What kinds of things does God want to accomplish through those who obey Him courageously—including you?
- How can you stand strong when someone says that what you believe about Jesus is just a myth or fairy tale?
- Dietrich Bonhoeffer faced terribly hard choices. It is easy to say what we might do, but think about being taken to jail or even beaten as a result of your faith. What Bible verses would you read and follow? What would you do and say?

truth in action

- Draft a "Family Statement of Faith." In one or two paragraphs, briefly summarize the truths of God's Word that your family believes and will stand on, no matter what anyone else says or does. Consider memorizing this statement of faith together or post it somewhere in your home, such as the refrigerator door or hallway, where family members can see it often and be reminded of the truth of the Christian faith.
- To find out more about the timeless truths that provide clear direction—and hope—for our future, read *The Family Manifesto*, available at FamilyLife.com or by calling 1-800-FL-TODAY.

praying together for truth

The One before whom we will stand, I pray You will help me remember the shortness of time and the nearness of eternity. May I never forget that Your eye always sees, that Your ear always hears, and Your heart of love always seeks to save. May I fulfill that which You have created me to do and stand firmly in the truth until my last breath. Amen.

daughter of the euphrates
truth inspires courage

What do Mount Ararat—where Noah's ark landed—and the Euphrates River have in common? Besides being mentioned in the Bible, they are located in the modern-day country of Turkey. And they were places familiar to a little girl named Elizabeth, who was born nearby.

Elizabeth and her family were Armenians, a people group who first heard the story of Jesus from His disciples, Bartholomew and Thaddaeus. More than two thousand years later, many of the people in Elizabeth's village were still following Christ. Elizabeth and her little sister learned the truths of the Bible from their mother and father. For them, these Bible stories were not just long-ago-and-far-away tales; they were part of their heritage.

Elizabeth's childhood was full of adventure and fun in spite of the growing knowledge she gained from listening to the adults speak of a massacre* that happened not long before she was born. Gradually she began to understand that Armenians were a minority in Turkey. Most of the other villages and cities nearby were populated by Turks. Elizabeth was learning to be cautious.

Your commandments make me wiser than my enemies, for they are ever mine.
—PSALM 119:98

These Bible stories were not just long-ago-and-far-away tales; they were part of their heritage.

When she was eleven, World War I began and with it the start of great suffering for Elizabeth's family and all Armenians.* In April 1915, her father was arrested and beaten by Turkish soldiers who accused him of crimes he did not commit.

When her father was released, a friend from a neighboring village came to visit. The two men talked while Elizabeth and her mother and sister waited in the next room. After the friend left, her father explained that their neighbor had offered them safety in his home if they would each renounce Christ and swear allegiance to Mohammad. For a long time they were silent. Then Elizabeth's mother began to sing softly, "What a friend we have in Jesus, all our sins and griefs to bear."[1] The truth about Jesus became their comfort.

Three days later her father was arrested again. Elizabeth was brave enough to sneak around buildings until she found him, badly beaten. On her knees, with her face near his, young Elizabeth heard her father's last words: "Never give up Christ no matter how much suffering might come.

Christ died for us. We can be as brave in His name."[2] Then a guard came and ordered her away. It was the last time she saw him.

During the night, Elizabeth, her sister, and their mother fled to the city. After arriving, her mother began going house to house, trying to find families who would take them as servants. This was her plan so that they might all three survive until the end of the war. But it was not to be.

Elizabeth was working as a servant in a Turkish home when she ran to her mother one afternoon and confessed the pressure she felt from her Turkish family wanting her to deny Christ. Her mother advised, "Remember your father's example," and then admitted, "My own time for facing that question has come. I was told today that all Armenian adults must acknowledge Mohammad or be exiled." She began crying and continued, "I cannot give up Christ, no matter how much you girls will need me. I cannot give Him up. I know that He will watch over you both."[3] After crying together, Elizabeth kissed her mother and ran back to her Turkish home.

The next day her mother was taken away, along with hundreds of other Armenians. Elizabeth and her sister were now orphans. Soon after, Elizabeth escaped from her Turkish masters, arriving days later at an American missionary hospital where she was allowed to stay if she would work.

Just twelve years old, Elizabeth labored alongside the doctors and nurses caring for hundreds of patients, most of them with war injuries. One day she tended a wounded Turkish soldier who asked about her family. She replied that she was an orphan, but as he persisted she told about her village, the death of her father, and their escape to the city. The soldier was silent, and then he said, "I killed your father. I have never forgotten. I am sick of killing."[4]

At first Elizabeth felt hatred for this man. Then she thought of her mother. What would she have done? What would she have said? Finally Elizabeth said softly, "Christ says we must forgive our enemies, and I forgive you." He replied, "Your Christ must be greater than Mohammad, since his teachings really live in your heart and life and are not merely remembered phrases."[5]

Elizabeth and her sister survived the war and came to live in America. The truth they learned from their parents gave them courage in unimaginable circumstances. Hopefully her story will inspire you to walk courageously in truth.

questions about truth

Many people claim to be brave, but we don't really know if they are until we see how they respond to challenges.

- What were some of the choices Elizabeth's family made because they believed the truth of Jesus?
- How does the truth inspire us to be courageous?

truth in action

- As a family, read more about Elizabeth's remarkable story in *Daughter of the Euphrates* (Paramus, NJ: The Armenian Missionary Assoc. of America, 1979).
- Go to *The Voice of the Martyrs'* website (www.persecution.com) to learn about people groups around the world who are being persecuted for their faith. Consider subscribing to their e-mail newsletter for weekly prayer updates.

praying together for truth

Father of the fatherless, not one of us is hidden from Your eyes. Not one of us is beyond Your reach. May we daily do as You instructed us and call upon Your name. And may we know Your loving care even in the midst of great loss, for it is always true. Amen.

TRUTH IN ACTION

date

Knowing truth is not enough. We need to live the truth, which means believing what God says and basing our actions and reactions on His Word. Sometimes this is easy to do, but sometimes it is difficult, requiring faith and bravery. As a family, list some of the truths that you believe and that you will base your life upon no matter what.

date

REFERENCE POINTS

DAY ONE: A **sextant** is an instrument used for measuring distances of latitude and longitude, especially helpful on large bodies of water. Today, many people use a GPS in a similar manner.

DAY TWO: Many of those who survived the hardships brought on by the **Indian Removal Act** eventually settled in what is now the state of Oklahoma.

DAY THREE: **Muslims** follow Islam, a religion based on the teachings of the prophet Mohammed. Muslims call their god *Allah*. Christians believe that Mohammed was a false prophet.

DAY FOUR: Martin Luther's list of reasons why the practice of **indulgences** was wrong was called the "95 Theses."

DAY FIVE: Many organizations exist today through which **sponsored children** are cared for. Your local church might be a good place to ask which organizations are available in your area.

DAY SIX: The Roman Colosseum is one famous arena where early Christians were **killed by wild animals**. People who die for their faith are called martyrs.

DAY SEVEN: A **massacre** is the act of killing many people at one time in an atrocious or cruel way. Many different massacres of the **Armenian** people have taken place throughout history.

notes

Day 1

1. Karen Loritts, telephone interview with the author, April 2011.
2. Ibid.

Day 2

1. Jeremiah Evarts quoted in Ebeneezer Tracy, *Memoir of the Life of Jeremiah Evarts* (Boston: Crocker and Brewster, 1845), 381.

Day 3

1. Mindy Belz, "Broadcast News," *World*, December 13, 2008, http://www.worldmag .com/articles/14763.
2. Ibid.

Day 4

1. Martin Luther quoted in Geoffrey Hanks, *70 Great Christians: The Story of the Christian Church* (Fearn, Scotland: Christian Focus, 2000), 107.

Day 5

1. UNICEF, 2008.
2. "Katie's Story," Amazima Ministries, accessed July 11, 2011, http://www.amazima .org/katiesstory.html.

3. Katie Davis, "Kisses from Katie," (blog), June 3, 2011, accessed July 11, 2011, http:// kissesfromkatie.blogspot.com/2011_06_01 _archive.html.

Day 6

1. Robert J. Morgan, *On This Day: 365 Amazing and Inspiring Stories about Saints, Martyrs and Heroes* (Nashville: Thomas Nelson, 1997), March 7.
2. Ibid.
3. Dietrich Bonhoeffer, *Letters and Papers from Prison* (New York: Simon and Schuster, 1997), 4.

Day 7

1. Elizabeth Caraman with William Lytton Payne, *Daughter of the Euphrates* (Paramus, NJ: The Armenian Missionary Association of America, Inc., 1979), 161.
2. Ibid., 197.
3. Ibid., 197–8.
4. Ibid., 236.
5. Ibid., 236–7.

photo credits

FRONT COVER

Cherokee woman—Cosand & Mosser, Denver Public Library

Old Bible—©iStockphoto.com (spaxiax)

Death march—http://en.wikipedia.org/wiki/File:Marcharmenians.jpg

Child—©iStockphoto.com (ranplett)

BACK COVER

Karen Loritts—Courtesy of Karen Loritts

Trail of Tears sign— http://en.wikipedia.org/wiki/Trail_of_Tears

Martin Luther—Lucas Cranach, Library of Congress

Sextant—©iStockphoto.com (Hadel Productions)

PAGE VI

Key on a page—©iStockphoto.com (Todd Arbini)

PAGE 2

Endurance ship—Used by permission of the Royal Geographical Society

Map—http://en.wikipedia.org/wiki/Imperial_Trans-Antarctic_Expedition

Old apartments—©Bigstock.com (Serge Horta)

Karen Loritts—Courtesy of Karen Loritts

PAGE 4

Sextant—©iStockphoto.com (Hadel Productions)

PAGE 6

Cherokee woman—Denver Public Library, Western History Collection, Cosand and Mosser.

The Trail of Tears, 1838 by Robert Lindneux—The Granger Collection

Trail of Tears sign—http://en.wikipedia.org/wiki/Trail_of_Tears

Jeremiah Evarts portrait—Used by permission of The New York Public Library

PAGE 8

Gavel and book—©iStockphoto.com (khz)

PAGE 10

Egypt—©iStockphoto.com (Juanmonino)

Father Zakaria Botross—Courtesy of the Botross family and CityHarvest Publications, Brisbane, Australia

Coptic Church—http://upload.wikimedia.org/wikipedia/commons/8/8c/Saint_Mark_Church%2C_Heliopolis.jpg

Lion—©iStockphoto.com (Andyworks)

PAGE 12

Satellite—©iStockphoto.com (1971yes)

PAGE 14

Martin Luther—Lucas Cranach, Library of Congress

Luther's writings—http://commons.wikimedia.org/wiki/File:LutherWritings&Portrait1581.jpg

Bounty Bible article—The New York Times

Lightning—©iStockphoto.com (filmstroem)

PAGE 16

Old lamp—©iStockphoto.com (Iguasu)

PAGE 18

Thomas Barnardo—IAM/akg

Orphan house—Copyright The Francis Frith Collection

Map—©bigstockphoto.com (rusak)

Katie Davis and child—Courtesy of Amazima Ministries International

PAGE 20

Bowl—©Kitsen | Dreamstime.com

PAGE 22

Dietrich Bonhoeffer— bpk, Berlin/Rotraut Forberg/Art Resource, NY

Bonhoeffer's home—bpk, Berlin/Stiftung Preussischer Kulturbesitz, SBB/Art Resource, NY

Hitler and soldiers—©bigstockphoto.com (kbuntu)

Nazi prison—©Micka | Dreamstime.com

PAGE 24

Old pitcher—©bigstockphoto.com (Marta Teron)

PAGE 26

Medieval church—©bigstockphoto.com (izuminka)

Armenian orphans—c1915, Library of Congress

Death march—http://en.wikipedia.org/wiki/File:Marcharmenians.jpg

Map—Public domain

PAGE 28

Old Bible—©iStockphoto.com (spaxiax)

PAGE 37

Barbara Rainey—J. E. Stover Photography, Inc.

A LETTER FROM THE AUTHOR

Dear Reader,

My husband and I had six children in ten years. The wide range of their ages and personalities made leading our children in any kind of home-centered spiritual direction a daunting task. So when a parent asks me how to encourage a fifteen-year-old in his faith while not ignoring the childlike questions of his five-year-old sister, I understand the predicament.

Where can a parent find stories and learning activities that are relevant to all ages? That was my dilemma; I could find no resources for a family like mine. I found lots of stories and songs for preschoolers and devotionals for teens, but nothing that would appeal to all of my children *together*.

What I did discover was that the best and easiest vehicle for transferring truth to my children was through stories. Whatever success we might have achieved in spiritually training our family came through shared stories of faith and discussions with our kids about taking God's truth with them into their lives. From that experience was born my dream to create resources to help moms and dads who want to be instrumental in raising children who are Christ followers.

Parents need something that works, something that is easy, something that requires no preparation. These seven stories make that possible. And unlike most devotional books that feature different themes with each day's reading, this resource focuses on one character quality that all parents want to develop in their children—truth. By reinforcing this one topic, my hope is that you and your family will grow in understanding what truth looks like and how to live accordingly.

Thanks for using this short family devotional. I pray that you and your children will grow together as you're inspired by the great faith of these men and women whose stories I've shared.

Barbara Rainey

ABOUT THE AUTHOR

Barbara Rainey is the mother of six adult children and the "Mimi" of seventeen grandchildren. She and her husband, Dennis, give leadership to FamilyLife, a ministry committed to helping marriages and families survive and thrive in our generation. Barbara has written several books, including *Thanksgiving: A Time to Remember, Barbara and Susan's Guide to the Empty Nest,* and *When Christmas Came.* The Raineys live in Little Rock, Arkansas. You can read more from Barbara online at FamilyLifeMomblog.com.

ABOUT THE SERIES

With captivating true stories to read as a family, these seven-day
interactive devotionals from speaker and best-selling author Barbara
Rainey saturate minds and hearts with memorable accounts and
vivid illustrations of true heroes who made noble choices.

Each day also includes:

- A key Bible verse

- Questions to discuss together

- A suggested prayer

- A personal record of your family's
  character as it relates to these stories

Encounter real-life heroes right in your living room—
and begin to grow together in character as a family.